CONSTITUTION

OF THE

State Historical Society of Iowa,

ADOPTED AT IOWA CITY,

February 7, 1857.

PRINTED BY JEROME & DUNCAN,

....

FEB. 22th, 1861.

CONSTITUTION

OF THE

State Historical Society of Iowa

ADOPTED AT IOWA CITY,

February 7, 1857.

PRINTED BY JEROME & DUNCAN,

....

FEB. 22th, 1861.

CONSTITUTION

OF THE

State Historical Society of Iowa,

CHAPTER I.

NAME.

ART. 1. This Organization shall be called the "State Historical Society of Iowa."

CHAPTER II.

MEMBERSHIP.

ART. 1. The members of this society shall consist of those persons who are elected at any meeting of the society, or by those officers authorized by this Constitution, and who pay into its treasury, annually, the sum of one dollar.

ART. 2. Individuals may be elected honorary members of this association, who shall be entitled to all the privileges of regular members, except the right to vote and hold office, and shall be exempt from paying the annual fee of membership.

ART. 3. The members of this society shall have free admission to its rooms and lectures, and the privilege of consulting its books, maps, charts and papers.

CHAPTER III.

OBJECT.

ART. 1. The object of this society, shall be to collect, embody, arrange and preserve in authentic form, a library of books, pamphlets, maps, charts, manuscripts, papers, paintings, statuary and other materials illustrative of the history of Iowa; to rescue from oblivion the memory of its early pioneers; to obtain and preserve narratives of their exploits, perils and hardy adventures; to secure facts and statements relative to the history, genius, progress or decay of our Indian tribes, to exhibibit faithfully the antiquities, and the past and present resources of the State; and to promote the study of history by lectures, and diffuse and publish information relating to the description and history of Iowa.

CHAPTER IV.

OFFICERS.

ART. 1. The officers of this society shall be a President, six Vice Presidents, a Corresponding Secretary, a Recording Secretary, a Treasurer, Librarian and eighteen Curators, who shall be chosen annually.

ART. 2. The President shall preside at the meetings of the association, preserve order therein, and in case of an equal division of the members, give the casting vote.

ART. 3. Either of the Vice Presidents, in the absence of the President, may perform the duties of that office.

ART. 4. The Recording Secretary shall keep a record of each meeting of the society, and submit the same for approval.

ART. 5. The Corresponding Secretary shall have charge of the correspondence of the society, be a member of the Board of Curators, have a general oversight of all its affairs, subject to the direction of the executive officers, to whom he shall make a monthly report of all his doings; write the annual report, and be known as the official organ.

ART. 6. The Treasurer shall receive all dues and donations of money, pay all drafts drawn on him when signed by the President and Secretary of the Board of Curators, and keep a regular account of the financial concerns of the society, and make a full and accurate report of the same, accompanied by satisfactory vouchors, to the Curators at their last regular meeting, previons to the annual meeting of the association.

ART. 7. The Curators; a majority of whom shall reside in the vicinity of the State University, and five of whom shall constitute a quorum, shall be the executive department of this association, having full power to manage its affairs in harmony with this constitution. They shall keep a full and correct account of all their doings, and make a report of the same, together with that of the Treasurer and Librarian of this society, through the Corresponding Secretary, at each annual meeting, to be transmitted to the Governor, and be by him laid before the General Assembly, as required by the act making an annual appropriation to this society. They shall also have the power, in the name of the State Historical Society of Iowa, for themselves and their successors in office, to sue and be sued, implead and be impleaded, defend and be defended in all courts and places, and for the purposes of this association may do all such acts as are performed by natural persons.

ART. 8. In case any vacancies occur in the officers

of this society, the Board of Curators shall have power to fill such vacancies, and also to elect such members of the society, as they may deem best, and appoint a corresponding member in each county.

Art. 9. The annual meeting of this society shall be held on the first Tuesday of December, at which time the officers for the succeeding year shall be chosen, and no member shall be eligible to an office, or be entitled to vote who has not paid the annual fee of membership.

Art. 10. The Librarian shall have charge of the books, papers, maps, charts and all other similar valuables of the society, under the direction of the Board of Curators, to whom he shall make report as they may require, to be by them incorporated in the annual report to the society.

CHAPTER V.

AMENDMENTS.

Art. 1. This constitution may be amended at any meeting of the society, when requested by the Board of Curators.

AMENDMENTS

CHAPTER I.

FEES OF MEMBERSHIP.

Art. 1. That membership shall hereafter require an initiation fee of five dollars, and an annual payment of one dollar.

ADDRESS TO THE PUBLIC,

BY ORDER OF THE BOARD OF CURATORS OF 1861.

A correct understanding of the real history of a community or people, is derived less, from an account of the *prominent* public transactions, than from a knowledge of the springs and influences which have wrought the changes, or led on to the event, or condition described.

It is not often, if ever, that any radical change of institution is effected, that any rapid growth or diminution of any of the material interests of the people is brought about, or any marked and decisive change in the social or moral aspect of affairs is produced, without a previously gradual and at the same time almost imperceptible modification of the circumstances and conditions upon which they were originally based. Revolutions, which are truly and permanently such, are seldom—never probably—the result of the seeming causes of their production—but slow, silent yet steady influences have been at work, which have wrought the real change in the elementary material of State or Community, long before the exciting cause which has produced its manifestation and public acknowledgment.

The same law must be conceded concerning marked changes in the status of communities, which become the subjects of the record of the chronicler. Unfortunately for each successive generation, the real history of its predecessors as thus described, has been transpiring so silently, and so little felt and appreciated by their participants, as to fail to attract the eye or pen of contemporaneous authors, until much of the most important material has passed from the reach of history.

It is in fact, often only by the light of final results that the full weight and importance of the acts or condition of a generation may be understood and measured

So likewise with its individuals, the men who set in motion a train of reform, or give out the suggestion that directs the public to the investigation, which leads to an important advancement in some aspect of its interests; or they who devise an improvement, or whose influence, (often of a local limit,) may have presented its claims to the public, are not often those who ride it into a notoriety that reaches to the time when the record of, by whom? by what means? or why? it was effected, becomes a matter of historical interest.

And yet these unconspicuous influences, these little facts of the passing hour, these half matured suggestions of the unheralded author, the individual exploit of the remote neighborhood, and a multitude of similar subjects, which have given shape, and tone, and direction to the public thought and mind; or laid the foundation upon which great public interests have been erected, are the real basis of its history—the real history of which,prominent incidents are but the manifestation.

If, as has sometimes been said, history is "philosophy teaching by example," then all the causes which have produced the example with their relative importance should be given, lest the philosophy taught should prove a false one.

To catch and hold these transpiring events, while yet fresh in the memory of their actors, or while they can be drawn from the pens of those personally cognizant of their occurrence, to lay in store the material, which shall give to those who come after us a truthful impression of every phase of condition, physical and moral; the thought, aspirations and hopes of the public mind; the ratio of progress; and whatever of particular in any of its concerns will give a true representation of the age, has come to be regarded as a matter of weighty importance by the present generation of our countrymen.

The dearth of facts concerning the Colonial and early State history of the elder States, and the feeling of the great need of these, by those who would study closely their history, led years ago to the establishment of Historical Societies, for the purpose of securing the objects alluded to. Their example has been followed with gratifying results, by States of more recent formation.

The young State of Iowa presents a fruitful field at the present time, for the collection of historical reminiscences, and calls imperatively for immediate effort in that direction. In this respect, it has peculiar claims for active and efficient work.

In no portion of our country, are the historic incidents of the past passing so rapidly from the knowledge of men, as here. An almost unexampled increase of its population from without, during the past ten years, and the rapid development of its vast resources by men "not of the manor born," and hence unfamiliar with the incidents of the early settlements—and pressing by their numerical power into relative nonim portance a large class of the men who laid the foundation of the Commonwealth, and won its early peaceful conquests, and sinking the public importance of the early times by the absorbing interest of the projects and enterprises of the ever fleeting present—while the time is rapidly passing which affords the opportunity of gathering the items of its early history from the few and widely separated sources of information remaining.

But there is another equally important consideration peculiar, in a measure, to our State. Iowa is now entering upon a career of experience, the conclusion of which may be of the highest importance to those of its own sons who shall come after, or to the world at large.

She has gathered from the treasures of the long and hard experience of the most advanced of *all* the others, and grouped them into a fabric of government, and shaped a course of policy, to be tried on a grander scale than ever before; and free from many of the prejudices and biases of the public mind, derivable from the usages and precedents, habits and traditional dogmas of the past of the older States, and which have there produced friction in their operations.

Without waiting the full fruition of experiment, she has caught the conclusions of her elder sisters; adopted their most liberal and comprehensive policies, planted fresh, deep, and expansive, on her bountiful soil the foundations of institutions from, and with improvements upon, their most perfect models; and Minerva like, has sprung full grown, in the breadth and depth of its policy, upon a career of action.

The world at large and especially Iowa's future citizens, have an interest in knowing the particulars of these beginnings, and of all the circumstances of their development from year to year, toward their culmination, provided they culminate in wealth and power, physical, and intellectual; or if on the other hand in any branch they prove a failure, the causes of such failure, or the want of adaptation of any institution or enterprise to the people or locality, should be held within the reach of the understanding of all.

Science also has a claim upon the present generation of our State, for the preservation of many of the species of its Natural History, natives of our forests, or prairies, or rivers, or brooks, or botanical varieties indigenous to our soil and climate, which are yearly disappearing.

The phenomena of our great prairies, with their meteorological relations, can never again so well be observed after the husbandman has "drove his plowshare" over its surface, and wrought the changes incident to the farm and homestead.

The claims of a race once its possessors, now disappearing, appeal to us to gather such of the history and traditions, and relics, as may be known to the present, or which will throw light upon their past. These must soon fade from the knowledge of men, unless collected and preserved by concerted effort on the part of those now in the active walks of life.

To this end, and to the promotion of other collateral interests of history and science, which the want of space forbids us to elaborate, has the State Historical Society of Iowa been established.

Through its agency, it is hoped that much which is valuable of incident or condition of the past may be gathered and held in reserve for the time when 'distance shall not only have lent its enchantment,' but when their bearings upon science, natural and political, and upon historic events *yet to transpire*, shall further enhance their importance.

How much may be done for the accomplishment of these objects, may be comprehended by a moment's view of an organization prosperously and thoroughly in operation. When it has secured the co-operation of our most intelligent and active citizens of all classes throughout all the sections of our great State. When a coterie of working members shall be enlisted in each of the hundred counties of the State, who will leave few events of either the past or present, untold. When "pioneers' from every locality shall be led to contribute their "experience" of early times. When men of science shall be laid under contribution for the result of their investigations or explorations in the various fields of scientific pursuit. When the researches of local antiquaries shall be directed to the collection of scattering remains and relics of the race gone before us. When the artist of the day shall lend his aid in preserving the scenes of historic interest, or catching the fleeting fashions of the hour, or the features of the men of whom the world has read or is yet to read. When the heads and authoritative powers of public and private institutions, shall be induced to explain the workings and progress of each. When copies of every publication, of whatever character, shall be secured. When last, but far from least, the newspapers of the whole State, those thermometers of social and political temperature, and chroniclers of the incidents of local interest of the passing hour, shall be received and preserved. When exchanges, with other States and other organizations, shall be effected, which shall bring to us the current concerns of other people than our own, throughout the civilized world.

Let all these be poured into a common reservoir, at a common center; systemized, classed, filed, recorded, and preserved. With judiciously directed efforts, what may a single generation alone accomplish for the truth of history and the cause of science.

It is to no less a consummation than that of which the outline is here faintly sketched, that all "to whom it may concern," throughout the State, are invited to lend a helping hand.

That the Society has not fallen behind the expectations of its friends thus far, will be apparent from a synopsis of its past brief history and its present condition, taken from the records, and from the reports of its executive officers.

The Society was organized during the winter of 1856-7. The organic act of the legislature of that session, placing it under the auspices of the State University, and granting an annual appropriation of $250 in aid of its objects.

The legislature of 1859-60, increased the appropriation to $500. Under this charter, and with this State aid the Society has been at work.

It has now a library of over 3,000 volumes, besides a large collection of pamphlets, and autograph letters of historical interest. Copies of all the maps of theState that have been published since its first settlement, one of which, of singular importance, dating back as early as 1650.

Photographs of a large number of the public men of the State, with several painted portraits of those who have been prominent in its early settlement. A cabinet of curiosities of the State. Choice specimens of its geology and natural history.

Histories written, or reliable promises of nearly one half the counties of the State.

Histories and traditions of some of the Indian tribes.

It is now in receipt of nearly one hundred newspapers, which are carefully preserved, and will in due time be bound.

It is in regular exchange with many kindred institutions of other States, to-wit: New Hampshire, Vermont, New York, Pennsylvania, Ohio, New Jersey, Connecticut, Maryland, Wisconsin, Minnesota, Illinois, Tennessee, Indiana, and other similar institutions of other States; and with a number of individuals of different countries. whose position is such as to enable them to promote materially the objects of the organization.

The officers of the Society, and those members resident in the vicinityof the Institution, are not as yet we believe open to any charge of want of zeal in forwarding its interests. The Annual Society Meetings have been well attended, and its condition and wants carefully examined, and measures harmoniously taken to further its objects. In no single instance have the monthly meetings of the Board of Curators been suspended for want of a quorum.

While its friends near the cen er of its operations, are thus active in promoting its welfare, it is to be hoped that its members, and other citizens of other portions of the State, having no less interest than they in its successs may give it a cordial support and helping hand in any of the great variety of ways which may be suggested to their minds by a careful consideration of the objects indicated.

SANFORD W. HUFF,
GEO. H. JEROME,
WM. REYNOLDS. } Committee.

IOWA CITY, Feb. 3d, 1861.

www.ingramcontent.com/pod-product-compliance
Lightning Source LLC
LaVergne TN
LVHW020637110826
845149LV00004B/1238

* 9 7 8 1 4 1 8 1 9 0 9 4 1 *